Beyond the School Gate

by

Kate Young

First published 2024 by The Hedgehog Poetry Press,

5 Coppack House, Churchill Avenue, Clevedon. BS21 6QW

www.hedgehogpress.co.uk

Copyright © Kate Young 2024

The right of Kate Young to be identified as the author of this work has been asserted in accordance with the Copyright, Designs and Patents Act 1988. All rights reserved. No part of this publication may be reproduced, stored in or introduced into a retrieval system, or transmitted in any form, or by any means (electronic, mechanical, photocopying, recording or otherwise) without prior written permissions of the publisher. Any person who does any unauthorised act in relation to this publication may be liable for criminal prosecution and civil claims for damages.

ISBN: 978-1-916830-25-7

Contents

First Song 7
Circle Time 8
What is Progress Anyway? 9
Closing the Gap 10
The Purest of Colours 12
Figure it Out 14
Inside Kai's Mind 15
Classroom 16
Miscalculation 18
Barricades 20
Faces of Angels 21
The Art Lesson 22
Acknowledgements 24

For all the inspirational teachers that have shaped my career and all the wonderful children I have had the pleasure to teach.

FIRST SONG

I secured my career with a pin in a map
and the ability to play the guitar,
its flat mahogany back a comfort
as I clattered the North Kent line through Strood
hurtling over the bridge to the classroom.

The stars were aligned, as they say,
good fortune on my side as I arrived
fresh faced, nervous but determined
to make a difference to every child
despite the cards that had been dealt.

Forty years on I read with hindsight,
interpret the shuffled suits wisely.
Eager eyes strain on the strings
as my fingers stroke new melody
noting the rhythm in each composition.

CIRCLE TIME

I am mining for gemstones.
Some children hold their gift close
loath to expose their shimmer
for fear of erosion or dimming.

Others keep it well hidden
in crevices or folds of stone
wary of failure or ridicule
when set against ringed gold.

It is my job to unearth each one
to polish the lustre in the centre.

WHAT IS PROGRESS ANYWAY?

She has a target.
It is time limited:
to write her name
Olivia
letters uniform
like soldiers on parade.

I know the **O**
is achievable.
She clenches
the chubby wax
with palm and claw
and circles appear
colossal and hollow.

V is a challenge,
all straight edges
and angles.
Its change of direction
reminds her
of playground games.

I call her mother in
to discuss progress.
The tiny chair
she squats on
makes her insignificant
I realise, embarrassed.

Tears fall as she
sees the letters wobble,
O the standout shape.
I'm sorry she blinks,
as a flood of pride
cascades between us.

CLOSING THE GAP

She slips in late
almost invisible to her peers
and settles herself.

The carpet square
absorbs the accident,
ammonia seeping into air.

I am aware of the subtle
shift of sticky bodies
inching to the edges,
noses in sleeves.
I divert attention,
ask to share her story.

She lifts the flap of her bag.
The stale stench of tobacco
and weed gush at nostrils
and I make a note to self:
fill in CPOMS
contact social worker.

Her limp hair hangs in strands
like greasy bacon rinds
and I want to wrap her
in the smell of spring mist
fresh from tumble-dried
sheets, clothing and love.

Dirtied nails trace phonemes,
pause on **O,** shape of the sun,
or the moon, or surprise
when her daddy comes home
and the room doesn't shout,
only holds its breath.

At five past three,
she drags her feet
to scuff away at time.

Later, I stare at data,
the need to *close the gap*.
Little pink lines diverge, widen.

THE PUREST OF COLOURS

A boy stares at a map of The Tube
looking for the blue line,
not the wavy blue of The Thames
but the blue that alights a flight of steps,
(no aeroplanes involved),
to Her Majesty's Theatre where he assumes
The Queen will be waiting to greet him.

The boy's eyes skitter anxiously
over three options as a confusion
of blue lines surface, swimming
Victoria   Piccadilly   DLR.
Three is not good, unlucky he thinks,
(he doesn't do shades, even in summer.)

'Tube', the boy rolls it under his tongue.
Singular. ***Tube: a hollow cylinder***
designed to squeeze him under London
from Point A to Point B. But the lines touch,
make contact then spin off at angles
to curious places like Oxford Circus
on the Red line, a gaudy-lipped clown.

The boy closes his eyes. Colours merge
as he rubs lids until kaleidoscopes form.
He considers the Brown of Bakerloo, (unsavoury),
the Yellow of Circle, (happy like a roundel sun,
though he doesn't do shades, even in summer),
the Black of the Northern to Charing Cross,
(he dislikes churches so it comes to pass).

A voice with no face slaps him squarely,
a boxer ringed in by claustrophobia.
This train terminates at ......, sounds fatal
as if the engine is dying on its wheels,
then a whoosh of warmth surprisingly menacing.
Mind the Gap, what does that mean?

Signage is misleading, personal even.
Gap: a break or hole between objects,
Mind: a person's ability to think.
The boy is often told he is different,
that the messages in his brain jump,
but he is perfect, this boy who stares at lines
and sees only the purest of colours.

FIGURE IT OUT

She tries to fit herself
into the class shaped hole
but the squeeze is too big,
muffled voice too loud
her echo, scream, mutter
oozing through tight walls,
flowing down
tunnel tapered corridors.

Someone places earmuffs
securely over her head
to protect her from the world,
a pilot preparing for take off
through another tight angled day,
runway littered with obstacles.

They think she is learning,
the specialists
as she feels her way through
soft curved spheres
and sharp-edged cubes,
gaining clarity
but her discerning eyes
see only the shapes between
the differences,
never the symmetry.

INSIDE KAI'S MIND

She tells me to pull my socks up
so I yank them up to my knees.
Do you think you're funny? she asks,
sometimes, I reply truthfully.

Her cheeks are like red pippins
when the skin is fit to burst
and that does make me laugh.
Red is my favourite colour.

She tells us to get undressed.
I don't know what P.E. stands for
but I do as I am told
though no one else is naked.

Don't get clever with me!
she screams, covering me up.
I thought that was the whole point,
you go to school to get clever.

Later, my head cool on the desk
a voice flaps *are you under the weather?*
No, I reply all matter-of-fact
I'm under the roof, weather's outside.

The pippins burst open.
Juice sprays all over my face.
She's too close, eyes locked in
so I scream, escape under the world.

CLASSROOM

The teacher wakes me with the usual
flick of a switch and my eyes
adjust to the artificial light.

I have a panoramic view over
the familiar landscape of desks
chairs, art pinned to my face.

She waters the plants on my sill
and carefully supports the stems
nurtured daily by young hands.

I listen to Enya's calm tones
absorbing the smoothness in my walls
and inhale the children's arrival.

We greet the small boy early
the skip of his step alarmingly bright
like a firecracker snaking the floor

and under his arm the 'bag for life'
bulges with disgust. He flips the contents
over my skin, the scrape of it burning.

Out spills a toothbrush, a pair of pjs
and a small brown bear
wrapped inside the change of clothes.

I observe the way his trauma spreads
like midnight ink on blotting, and think:
six placements in eighteen months.

I accept the knuckle of abuse
the swift cut and punch to plaster
my paint cracked by his rage.

I feel the grip of his toes on my sill
hear the snap of healthy stems
green sap staining his palm.

Home Time. The hours tick by.
Gone six, we wait at my door
listen to rainfall. No one comes.

MISCALCULATION

Lately, she's been drifting into school
like a waning moon
pale-faced and full of excuses.
The smudges over her cheek bones
deepen the pit of her eyes
grey as hollowed craters.

Sleepless nights
escaping aliens
over an i-pad screen?

But now, as I haul myself
through the long wade
of parent's evening
I catch her in a new light,
wiry frame struggling to steer
the cumbersome chair into class.

Eventually, I compose myself
and smile, the pull of understanding
stretched wide.

How's she doing?
She finds the mornings hard,
sorry if sometimes she's late.

The words are slurred,
floating in space
like pieces of disembodied debris.
MND Beth mouths silently
planting a foot
safely on the brake.

I revise my report,
quickly adjust my tone
to fit around the kindest of lies,
she's doing just fine.
Then, *Beth is a truly caring child.*
I am mortified, make my correction.

BARRICADES

Snail-like, he slopes into class
rucksack on his back
and unpacks his anger on the desk.

He keeps the weight of his home
close to his body
like an unexploded shell

leaving a howl of devastation
in his wake
while I assess the risk

the frown-furrow in fields of skin,
the tick of a knuckle-white fist,
the mouth like an oval scream.

He sneaks a glance at the boy
who slips in late
and takes his place in the corner.

This child carries nothing,
his face a blank emoji,
when I call his name, he is mute.

I note the curl of his hurt
as he slithers into himself
and locks the door behind him.

They don't all shout and scream.

FACES OF ANGELS

Watching her tear shapes
from folded paper
she is oblivious to her peers,
a study in concentration

all dimpled cheeks
and naive eyes,
a child's key to ensure
they will be loved.

She unfolds her snowflake,
disappointment falls to the floor
with snippets of tissue
and tears of frustration.

I cup my hand over hers
so the scissors glide smoothly,
her tongue clipping her lip
to the rhythm of the blade.

In time we open her craft,
it unfolds with her smile
into something precious
unique, like all the others.

We hang them from strings
criss-crossing the classroom,
thirty angel faces look up,
halo-mouths speechless.

THE ART LESSON

On the last day of term
a bouquet arrives
along with a card
and a beautifully painted scene
of an oast house,
slightly off-kilter
but remarkably skilled
for one so young.

It is a thank you
for letting him dream
and doodle through Maths
while I turned a blind eye
providing the means
and encouragement.

I am touched by the gesture,
wonder if in twenty years
I will spot his unique blend
of colour and tone
as I browse the art
in the Summer Exhibition
of the Royal Academy
and remember the boy

slightly off-kilter

ACKNOWLEDGEMENTS

Figure it Out and *The Purest of Colours* were first published by The Ekphrastic Review. *Inside Kai's Mind* and *Barricades* have appeared in Dreich magazine. *Barricades* has also been published in Openings 40, an anthology by OU Poets. *Faces of Angels* has been published by The Poet.

My thanks go to the many poets who have supported me with the process of writing- the Mid-Kent stanza and the members of the Open University Poets. Also, a huge thank you to Mark at Hedgehog Press who has worked tirelessly to publish this, and many other poetry pamphlets.

www.ingramcontent.com/pod-product-compliance
Lightning Source LLC
Chambersburg PA
CBHW030313100526
44590CB00012B/632